THE

MAGNIFICENT
BOOK OF TREASURES

ANCIENT
ROME

THE
MAGNIFICENT
BOOK OF TREASURES
ANCIENT
ROME

ILLUSTRATED BY **EUGENIA NOBATI**
WRITTEN BY **STELLA CALDWELL**

weldon**owen**

Written by Stella Caldwell
Illustrated by Eugenia Nobati
Consultant: Dr Ben Salisbury

weldon**owen**

Published by Weldon Owen Children's Books
An imprint of Weldon Owen International, L.P.
A subsidiary of Insight International, L.P.
PO Box 3088
San Rafael, CA 94912
www.insighteditions.com

Weldon Owen Children's Books:
Designer: Karen Wilks
Editor: George Maudsley
Assistant Editor: Pandita Geary
Senior Production Manager: Greg Steffen
Art Director: Stuart Smith
Publisher: Sue Grabham

Insight Editions:
Publisher: Raoul Goff

A CIP catalogue record for this book is available
from the British Library.

ISBN: 978-1-68188-744-9

Manufactured, printed, and assembled in Turkey.
First printing, LEV0522
10 9 8 7 6 5 4 3 2 1

INTRODUCTION

Legend tells that the city of Rome was founded by twin brothers Romulus and Remus in 753 BCE. At that time, Rome was just a tiny settlement. But over the course of a thousand years, it became a vast empire that stretched all the way from England to Egypt. In fact, it was one of the greatest civilizations the world has ever known. The Romans were brilliant builders, engineers, inventors, and artists. They introduced new ideas and ways of living, and created beautiful objects that we can still admire today.

The Magnificent Book of Treasures Ancient Rome takes you on a spectacular journey through this fascinating world and its wonderful riches. Be amazed at a gladiator's gleaming helmet and imagine what it was like to fight in a great arena. Meet powerful emperors such as Marcus Aurelius and famous empresses such as Livia Drusilla. Read about the god of war, Mars, the snake-haired monster, Medusa, and the goddess of chance, Tutela.

Find out about the mighty Roman army and admire a soldier's shield and sword. Learn how the city of Pompeii was destroyed by a volcano and see the glinting serpent bracelet found buried in its ruins. Marvel at a clever eating tool, a mosaic showing a chariot race, and an extraordinary theater mask.

Travel back in time to the heart of ancient Rome to discover some of its most magnificent treasures.

FACT FILE

Discovered: Hawara, Egypt

Found today: Cleveland Museum of Art, Cleveland, Ohio, USA

Date: Around 25–37 CE

Materials: Wood, beeswax, colored pigment, gold leaf

Size: 15½ in (39.4 cm) high, 6¾ in (17.4 cm) wide

CONTENTS

THE GOLDEN EAGLE

🏛 The eagle was an important symbol in the Roman world. It stood for strength, courage, and victory.

🏛 The Roman army was divided into legions. Every legion had its own standard, which was a pole with a bronze eagle, or *aquila*, perched on the top. The *aquila* was proudly carried into battle and protected at all costs.

🏛 The bird's outstretched wings stood for the Roman Empire's great power. At its height, the empire stretched from England to Egypt.

🏛 The eagle holds a wreath made from the leaves of a laurel tree in its beak. Laurel wreaths were a sign of success to the Romans. Victorious generals wore laurel crowns to mark their triumph in battle.

🏛 The bodies of dead emperors were burned in funeral pyres. As the flames crackled, a caged eagle was set free to carry the emperor's soul up to the heavens.

🏛 The god of the sky and thunder, Jupiter, is often pictured with an eagle at his side. The bird was his trusted companion and messenger.

FACT FILE

Discovered: Sisak, Croatia

Found today: Archaeological Museum, Zagreb, Croatia

Date: 100–300 CE

Materials: Bronze

Size: 9 in (23 cm) high

WILD BEAST HUNTER

- A courageous hunter confronts a fierce lioness in a packed amphitheater. He uses all his skill and experience to kill the wild animal quickly.

- The man is a type of gladiator known as a *venator*. *Venatores* were expert hunters who killed wild beasts for public entertainment.

- The Romans brought ferocious animals from all over their empire for gladiator shows—lions, bears, tigers, elephants, hippos, wild boar, and even crocodiles.

- The hunter shows his bravery by using just a padded armguard as protection. His only weapon is his spear.

- Sometimes wild animals jumped across barriers and safety ditches into the audience, attacking spectators.

- This wall painting was discovered at a giant stadium that could hold 15,000 people. Special guests sat in boxes and enjoyed the best views.

- Unarmed prisoners also faced terrifying animals in the arena. They would be savaged and killed by the beasts as the crowds cheered.

Discovered: Mérida, Spain

Found today: National Museum of Roman Art, Mérida, Spain

Date: 67–100 CE

Materials: Granite, lime mortar, stucco

Size: 25¼ in (64 cm) high, 40½ in (103 cm) wide

THE SOLDIER'S SHIELD

- A legionary, or foot soldier, carried this decorated shield into battle for protection.

- A Roman curved shield is called a *scutum*. This one was found in 13 pieces, and is the only one that still exists.

- The shield was light enough to be held with one hand. A soldier could raise it up to cover their body while using their other hand to swing a sword.

- This shield was dug up at the ancient city of Dura-Europos in Syria. The Romans captured the city nearly 2,000 years ago.

- An iron knob once covered the hole in the middle of the shield. It was called a boss. A soldier could punch an enemy with the boss, knocking them off balance.

- Roman soldiers sometimes defended themselves by forming a tortoise shape. Soldiers at the front locked their shields together while others held them over their heads to make a protective shell.

- The eagle at the top of this shield is perched on a globe. This was a sign of Roman power.

- The winged figures to either side of the eagle are 'victories' and represent success in battle.

- The lion at the shield's base is a figure of strength. It might have reminded a soldier of the great hero Hercules, who famously killed a lion with his bare hands.

FACT FILE

Discovered: Site of Dura-Europos, Syria

Found today: Yale University Art Gallery, New Haven, Connecticut, USA

Date: About 250 CE

Materials: Painted wood, animal hide

Size: 41½ in (105.5 cm) high, 16¼ in (41 cm) wide, 11¾ in (30 cm) deep

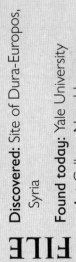

13

MEDUSA'S STARE

🏛 The Romans told stories of a terrifying monster called Medusa. Her hair was a mass of hissing snakes, and her horrifying stare could turn an onlooker to stone.

🏛 Medusa was one of three dreadful sisters called the Gorgons. Here, her hypnotizing eyes are shown in silver, and two serpents wriggle from beneath her flowing hair.

🏛 The Romans celebrated great battle victories with a ceremony called a triumph. Successful generals were paraded through the streets in a special chariot pulled by four horses. Medusa may once have decorated one of the chariots.

🏛 Medusa's face was used in Roman art as a symbol of protection. People believed it could keep away evil spirits.

🏛 The carving is mainly made from bronze. Roman blacksmiths mixed copper and tin to create this material.

🏛 Medusa was slain by the great hero Perseus. He sliced off her head as she slept in a cave. Later, he gave Medusa's head to the goddess of war and wisdom, Minerva.

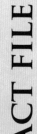

FACT FILE

Discovered: Lake of Albano, Lazio, Italy

Found today: Metropolitan Museum of Art, New York City, USA

Date: 1–200 CE

Materials: Bronze, silver, copper

Size: 7¼ in (18.3 cm) high, 7 in (17.9 cm) wide, 4¼ in (10.7 cm) deep

15

GARDEN OF PLENTY

🏛 Birdsong and the scent of flowers and fruit fill a lush garden. This wall painting, or fresco, decorated the dining room of a luxurious Roman villa.

🏛 The painting is part of a garden scene that ran around the dining room's four walls. The room was half underground to keep it cool. Guests could imagine they were outside in a large, beautiful garden.

🏛 The villa belonged to Livia Drusilla. She was the third wife of Rome's first emperor, Augustus. She used her underground garden room to host luxurious banquets for the empire's most important people.

The Romans ate a lot of fruit. To the left of this scene is a tree full of golden quince fruit. On the right, there is a tree full of juicy red pomegranates.

There are several small laurel trees in the painting. Their leaves were used to make laurel crowns for emperors.

The scene is full of birds. A pheasant sits on the wall and a blackbird flaps through the blue sky. The black-and-yellow bird perched in a tree is a rare golden oriole.

FACT FILE

Discovered: Prima Porta, Italy

Found today: National Roman Museum, Rome, Italy

Date: 30–20 BCE

Materials: Paint, plaster

Size: 19 ft 4 in (5.9 m) wide

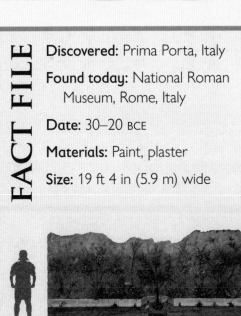

THE GOLDEN SERPENT

🏛 A coiled snake glitters with gold. To the ancient Romans, serpents were symbols of good fortune, and not something to be feared. This bracelet may have made its owner feel safe and protected.

🏛 The gold bracelet belonged to a wealthy woman. It was placed on the upper arm. Bracelets were often worn in pairs, one on each wrist or arm.

🏛 Roman women wore necklaces, earrings, rings, and bracelets. Roman men wore jewelry, too, and often had several rings on their fingers.

🏛 Harmless snakes were frequently kept by the Romans as pets. They helped to keep houses free of pests by eating mice and other rodents.

🏛 The Romans were skilled metalworkers, and made many useful tools, weapons and ornate jewelry. They mined the metals they needed, including copper, iron, tin, silver, and gold, from all over the empire.

🏛 This bracelet was found in the ruins of Pompeii. The city was buried in ash after the colossal eruption of the volcano Vesuvius. Archaeologists discovered jewelry still on the skeletons of some of the victims.

FACT FILE

Discovered: Pompeii, Italy

Found today: National Archaeological Museum, Naples, Italy

Date: About 50 CE

Materials: Gold

Size: 3½ in (8.8 cm) wide, 1¼ in (3 cm) deep

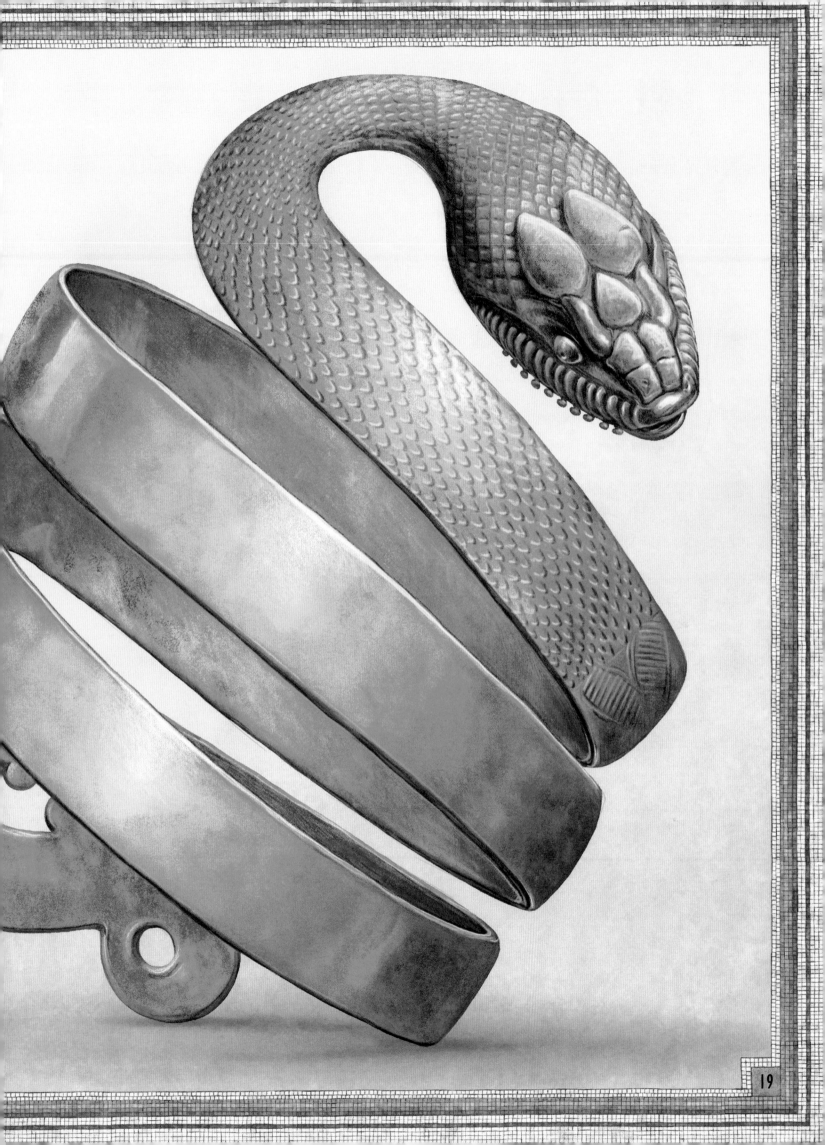

The Seafloor

This mosaic decorated the floor of a seaside Roman villa. The busy scene shows lots of different types of fish, including bream, mullet, sea bass, and snapper. The people who lived in this villa ate these fish as part of their diet.

The mosaic is made of small pieces of stone and glass. Mosaic floors were laid in public buildings and the homes of wealthy people.

Workers accidentally discovered the mosaic floor when they were widening a city street. Unusually, it was in almost perfect condition.

- The huge fish with the long, curly tail is probably meant to be a whale. It looks like it is about to devour one of the ships.

- The two ships in the scene were used for trade. They carried grains, spices, and other goods around the empire.

- Beneath the villa floor, archaeologists discovered the 1,700-year-old footprints of the mosaic's artists.

FACT FILE

Discovered: Lod, Israel

Found today: Shelby White and Leon Levy Lod Mosaic Archaeological Center, Lod, Israel

Date: About 300 CE

Materials: Colored limestone and glass

Size: Approx. 13 ft (4 m) wide

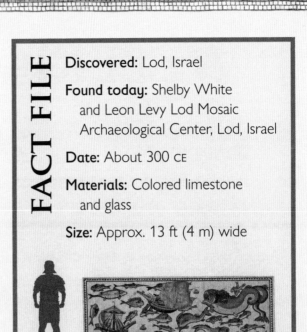

JEWELED DAGGER

This precious dagger was discovered in a Roman soldier's grave. It was still in its sheath, or scabbard, and was covered in a thick layer of rust. Archaeologists cleaned and treated it for several months until it shone like it did 2,000 years ago.

The dagger probably belonged to a legionary or an officer serving in the Roman army. Roman soldiers weren't usually buried with their weapons, so it is a mystery why this dagger was left with its owner.

FACT FILE

Discovered: Haltern am See, Germany

Found today: Roman Museum, Haltern am See, Germany

Date: About 9 CE

Materials: Silver, brass, iron, linden wood, niello, enamel, glass

Size: 13 in (33 cm) long

The dagger was found in the Teutoburg Forest, which is in present-day Germany. Fifteen thousand Roman soldiers were killed in battle there. It was a terrible defeat for the Roman army.

Part of a matching belt was unearthed with the dagger. The four rings on the dagger's sheath were used to attach the weapon to the owner's belt.

The dagger's iron handle is inlaid with silver and red glass. The iron scabbard is lined with wood, and decorated with silver, glass, and enamel.

A Roman soldier's main weapon in battle was a sword. He used a dagger if he lost his sword, or if it became damaged.

DOUBLE PORTRAIT

🏛 This double portrait was painted on the inside wall of a house in Pompeii. A man called Terentius Neo poses alongside his wife. Experts think he was probably a baker because part of his house was used as a bakery.

🏛 This painting is a fresco, which means "fresh" in Italian. Roman fresco artists painted straight onto fresh, wet plaster. They had to work quickly before the plaster dried.

🏛 The woman clutches a wax tablet made from wood and beeswax in her left hand. The Romans used the tablets as reusable writing pads. The pointed stylus in her right hand was for writing on the wax.

🏛 The man is wearing a white piece of clothing called a toga. He is holding a papyrus scroll. The Romans used papyrus paper, made from the Egyptian papyrus plant, for their special documents.

🏛 In Roman society, women usually came second to men. But in this portrait, the man and woman are treated as equals. In fact, the woman is slightly in front of her husband, making her look more important.

FACT FILE

Discovered: Pompeii, Italy

Found today: National Archaeological Museum, Naples, Italy

Date: 55–79 CE

Materials: Paint on plaster

Size: 25½ in (65 cm) high, 22¾ in (58 cm) wide

AT THE RACES

- Galloping hooves thunder and the crowd roars as chariots hurtle round the track. Four chariots, each pulled by four horses, compete in the race shown in this mosaic.

- Chariot racing was one of the most popular sports in the Roman Empire, but it was extremely risky. There were many crashes, and drivers and horses were sometimes killed. This only added to the excitement of the audience.

- This mosaic shows a huge stadium called the Circus of Carthage. It had space for 60,000 spectators. They came and went through the doorways in the stadium wall.

- There were four main chariot teams. They were the Blues, the Greens, the Reds, and the Whites. Roman fans cheered for their favorite team in the same way that sports fans do today.

- The starting gates are at the right of the racetrack. When an official dropped a white flag, the gates sprung open and the race began.

- The long, low wall down the center of the racetrack is called the *spina*. It is decorated with sculptures that could be tilted to show spectators how many laps had been completed.

- The man holding a jug is called a *spasore*, or sprinkler. His job was to throw water over the sprinting horses to help cool them down. He needed to be brave because it was a dangerous task!

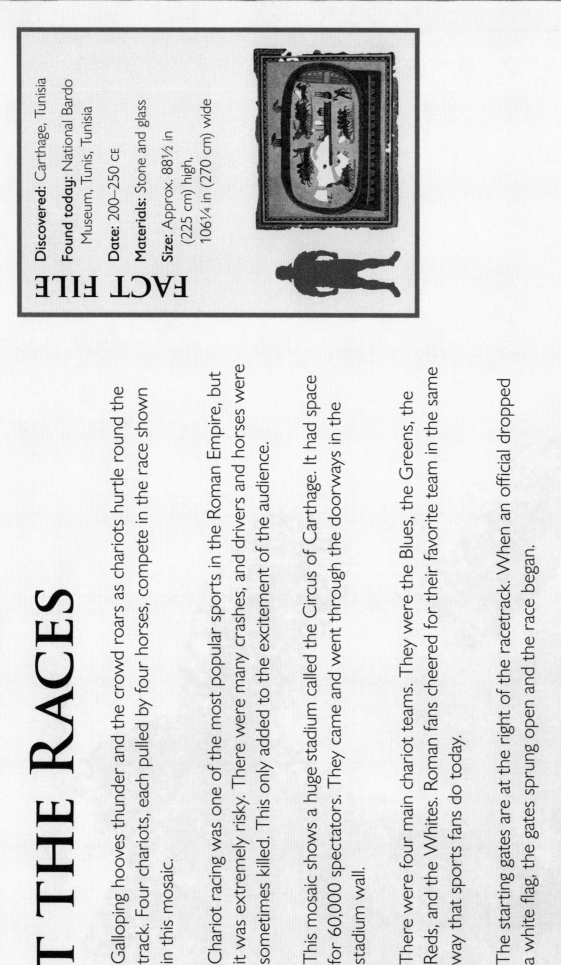

FACT FILE

Discovered: Carthage, Tunisia

Found today: National Bardo Museum, Tunis, Tunisia

Date: 200–250 CE

Materials: Stone and glass

Size: Approx. 88½ in (225 cm) high, 106¼ in (270 cm) wide

LEATHER BOOT

- This leather boot was worn by someone living in Londinium (modern-day London, UK), on the edge of the Roman world. It was preserved in the soft mud of the river Thames for nearly 2,000 years before it was found.

- This was a fashionable boot. The Romans preferred sturdier shoes and boots for outdoor work and in cold, wet weather. Light sandals were worn at home, as well as in the summer months.

- The boot's leather laces have not survived. They were once threaded through the little flaps running along the top.

- Some types of outdoor shoes were lined with studs called hobnails. These made them strong and gave them better grip. Roman soldiers wore hobnailed sandal-boots, or *caligae*, which could survive many days of marching.

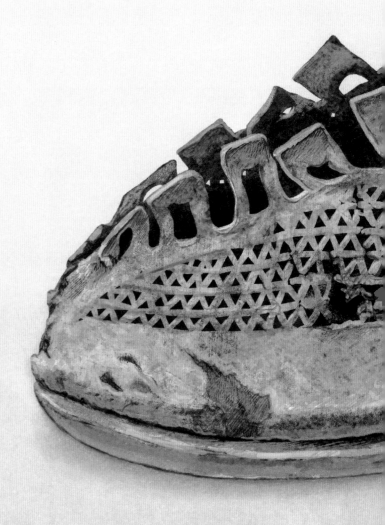

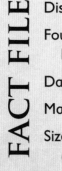
FACT FILE

Discovered: River Thames, London, UK

Found today: Museum of London, London, UK

Date: 70 CE

Materials: Leather

Size: 10¼ in (26.2 cm) long, 3¾ in (9.8 cm) high, 3¼ in (8 cm) wide

This intricate pattern of cut-out holes allowed the wearer's colored stockings to show through.

The Romans were skilled tanners, or leather makers. They used cow and goat skin to make leather boots, shoes, shields, belts, horse straps, and reins. Leather workshops, or tanneries, were located out of town because of their unpleasant smell.

GLADIATOR'S HELMET

FACT FILE

Discovered: Pompeii, Italy

Found today: British Museum, London, UK

Date: 1–100 CE

Materials: Bronze

Size: 19 in (48.3 cm) high

A gladiator once wore this bronze helmet. This trained fighter took part in violent contests against other gladiators or wild animals in front of huge crowds.

The gladiator wearing this helmet fought with a sword or dagger and a shield. His limbs were protected by padded leather or metal guards.

The fighter looked at his enemy through the linked holes at the front of the helmet. The holes were very small, so he would have struggled to see clearly.

The large flaps around the bottom of the helmet covered the gladiator's throat and the back of the neck. The helmet was very heavy, so it was difficult for him to move around quickly.

The large crest was for show. Feathers or plumes of horsehair were used to decorate it.

There is a carving of Hercules beneath the helmet's crest. This mythical Roman hero was famous for his incredible strength.

THE VOYAGE OF ULYSSES

🏛 The mythical king Ulysses stands chained to a ship's mast in this carving. Ulysses was the Roman name for the ancient Greek king Odysseus. The Romans adopted many of their gods and myths from the Greeks.

🏛 In myths, the Sirens were dangerous creatures who were half woman, half bird. They sang enchanting songs to lure sailors to their deaths. In this scene, Ulysses has asked his crewmates to tie him to the ship's mast so he can hear the music and survive.

🏛 Ulysses was a brave warrior who fought in a great war against the city of Troy. This carved panel, or relief, tells one of the many stories about his long sea voyage home to Greece.

🏛 This relief probably once decorated a tomb. Scenes from popular myths were often displayed on Roman tombs. Sometimes the images showed hunting or battle scenes, or details from the life of the dead person.

FACT FILE

Discovered: Campania, Italy

Found today: Louvre Museum, Paris, France

Date: 100–200 CE

Materials: Terracotta

Size: 12¾ in (32.5 cm) high, 16 in (40.5 cm) wide

The carving is made of terracotta, which is clay baked at a very high temperature. The Romans also used terracotta for bricks, tiles, pottery, and building decoration.

The story in this carving is told in a famous poem called *The Odyssey*. It was written by an ancient Greek author and poet called Homer.

PAINTED BEDROOM

■ This fresco decorated a bedroom wall in a country villa near the city of Pompeii. It was preserved in ash after the catastrophic eruption of Mount Vesuvius in 79 CE.

■ The painting has four panels, which each contain a scene. They show views of buildings along a street. If you were standing in the room, you might feel as if you were looking through a window to the outside world.

■ The colors of a painting often changed as a fresco dried, so the artist had to wait to see how their work turned out.

■ This painting's skillful artist wanted to play tricks on their audience. A small, slanted square roof in the first scene makes you feel as if you are looking down on it from above. But the nearby balcony is painted as if you are looking up from the street below!

The second scene shows a small temple known as a shrine. The gold statue is the goddess of witchcraft, Hecate. Above her is a mask of the woodland god Silenus.

The first and third panels show the same scene. They are mirrored reflections of each other.

There is a round temple in the final scene. The Romans built grand temples to worship their many gods and goddesses. Religion was an important part of Roman life.

FACT FILE

Discovered: Boscoreale, Italy

Found today: Metropolitan Museum of Art, New York City, USA

Date: 50–40 BCE

Materials: Paint on plaster

Size: 8 ft 8 in (2.65 m) high, 19 ft 2 in (5.84 m) wide

CAVALRY MASK

This bronze helmet was once worn by a member of the cavalry—a Roman soldier who fought on horseback.

The helmet was not worn to fight in real battles. It was a sports mask used in tournaments and mock battles. Cavalry soldiers practiced their riding and fighting skills at these huge events.

The soldier who owned this mask wore a brightly colored tunic and carried a long sword or spear. Their lower legs were protected with shin armor called greaves.

A name is scratched inside the helmet. It is thought to be Marcianus.

There are two men and three women at the top of the mask. Experts think they are connected to Bacchus, the god of wine and pleasure.

The hinge below the row of people at the top let the soldier lower or raise the face mask. The rim at the bottom of the helmet covered their neck.

The mask is made of bronze with a thin layer of shining silver. The lips and eyelids are coated with gold leaf. The helmet also had an iron cap that fitted around the skull, but most of it has worn away.

FACT FILE

Discovered: Nijmegen, Netherlands

Found today: Valkhof Museum, Nijmegen, Netherlands

Date: 50–100 CE

Materials: Bronze, iron, silver, gold leaf

Size: 9½ in (24.2 cm) high

THE WISE EMPEROR

- Marcus Aurelius was one of Rome's most successful emperors. His reign brought great prosperity to the empire. This magnificent bronze statue honors him as a wise and noble leader.

- The statue probably stood in the Forum, the public square at the heart of Roman life.

- The emperor carries no weapons. He is shown as a bringer of peace rather than as a great warrior.

- The statue was once covered in shining gold leaf. Most of it has worn away, but you can still see traces of gold on the sculpture's surface.

- This is the only surviving bronze sculpture of a Roman emperor on horseback. Many others were made, but were melted down to reuse their metal.

- Marcus Aurelius stretches out his right arm as if speaking to a vast crowd. He is made to look slightly larger on his horse than he would really have been. This helps show his grandeur and power.

■ Large, bronze statues were difficult to make. This one was probably created as several smaller pieces that were then skillfully joined together.

■ Marcus Aurelius was also a great thinker, or philosopher. He recorded his ideas about the importance of duty, hard work, and responsibility.

FAST FOOD BAR

Two thousand years ago, people in Pompeii bought fast food from this snack bar, or *thermopolium*. Street food was very popular in Roman times. More than 80 snack bars have been found in Pompeii alone.

Many Romans could not afford to have a kitchen at home. Buying food from a street bar like this was quick and easy. You can imagine people chatting around the bar as they ate.

The fast-food counter had deep jars to store hot food and drinks. The remains of snails, pig, goat, and fish were discovered in them.

Colorful pictures decorate the sides of the counter. The two dead ducks and the rooster probably advertised the duck and chicken on the menu. Archaeologists uncovered a piece of a duck bone near the bar.

There is a painting of a leashed dog to the side of the counter. It might have warned customers to keep their pet dogs under control.

Experts dug up jars for cooking stews and soup near the bar. They also unearthed a wine flask and a bronze drinking bowl.

The bones of at least two people were found near the snack bar. One of them may have been the owner, killed in the volcanic eruption that destroyed Pompeii.

RULER OF OCEANS

🏛 Myths tell of how the powerful water god Oceanus created the first oceans and seas. He, his wife Tethys, and their many children ruled over the world's streams, lakes, and springs. This fabulous metal mask shows the face of Oceanus in all his glory.

🏛 This mask once decorated a water fountain in the grounds of a grand villa. Jets of water gushed through the god's open mouth.

🏛 Fish scales cover the water god's face. All kinds of sea creatures dance through his curly hair and beard.

🏛 The Romans had ingenious ways of supplying clean water to their cities. Large stone channels called aqueducts carried water from springs and streams to storage tanks. Lead pipes then took the water to public fountains and baths, and to some homes.

🏛 Public fountains were an important part of any Roman town or city. Most people collected their water from them using a bucket. Wealthy people often had impressive fountains in their gardens and courtyards.

🏛 The Romans believed their gods had the power to punish them or to send them good luck. The face of Oceanus on this fountain mask reminded people to thank him for his gift of water.

FACT FILE

Discovered: Near Treuchtlingen, Germany

Found today: Bavarian State Archaeological Collection, Munich, Germany

Date: 200–235 CE

Materials: Bronze, copper, silver

Size: 6¾ in (17.3 cm) wide

ROMULUS AND REMUS

■ Myths tell how the great city of Rome was founded by the twin brothers Romulus and Remus. This mosaic shows them as babies beneath a large female wolf.

■ Legend has it that the twin boys were looked after by the wolf in this scene. She raised them as her own children after they were abandoned by their parents.

■ The wolf seems to have the body of a horse. Perhaps the artist had never seen a real wolf.

■ In the story, Romulus and Remus disagreed about where to build a new city. They fought, and Romulus killed his brother. He then called the city Rome, naming it after himself.

■ Mosaics have been found all over the Roman world. They were made from thousands of tiny colored stones, and often showed images from famous myths like this one. Hunting scenes and fighting gladiators were also popular subjects.

FACT FILE

Discovered: Aldborough, UK

Found today: Leeds City Museum, Leeds, UK

Date: 300–400 CE

Materials: Stone

Size: 55 in (140 cm) high, 55 in (140 cm) wide

POCKET EATING TOOL

🏛 This clever tool is a little bit like a modern Swiss Army knife. It has many useful parts, including a spoon and a fork. It once had an iron knife, too, but this rusted and has worn away.

🏛 Each tool folds in and out of the central section.

🏛 The tool's owner may have used the long spike to scoop out the flesh of snails. The Romans loved eating snails. They fattened them up on milk and bran in special gardens.

🏛 Next to the long spike is a tool with a tiny spoon at the end. It might have been used as a toothpick, or to scoop out earwax.

🏛 The Romans hardly ever used knives and forks at the table. Instead, they used spoons or their hands for eating food.

🏛 This tool is unusual not only because of its folding parts but also because it is mainly made from silver. Many Roman knife-spoons were made from bronze.

- Experts think the little hooked tool may have been used to scrape sauce out of a narrow-necked bottle.

- The folding tool was a luxury item, but it was also practical. It would have come in useful for wealthy travelers.

FACT FILE

Discovered: The Mediterranean area

Found today: Fitzwilliam Museum, Cambridge, UK

Date: 201–300 CE

Materials: Silver, iron

Size: 3½ in (8.8 cm) high, 6 in (15.5 cm) long

ROMAN MUMMY

- This portrait is of a teenage girl. She lived in Egypt when it was part of the Roman Empire. After she died, her body was mummified and this painting was placed on the mummy's head.

- The girl lived during the reign of the second Roman emperor, Tiberius. Historians know this because her hairstyle was fashionable at that time.

- The mummy portrait lay buried for almost 2,000 years. The colors are still bright because the dry heat of Egypt preserved the paint.

- The artist used paint made from beeswax and colored pigment. The portrait was painted onto a wooden board, which was attached to the mummy's head with a linen bandage.

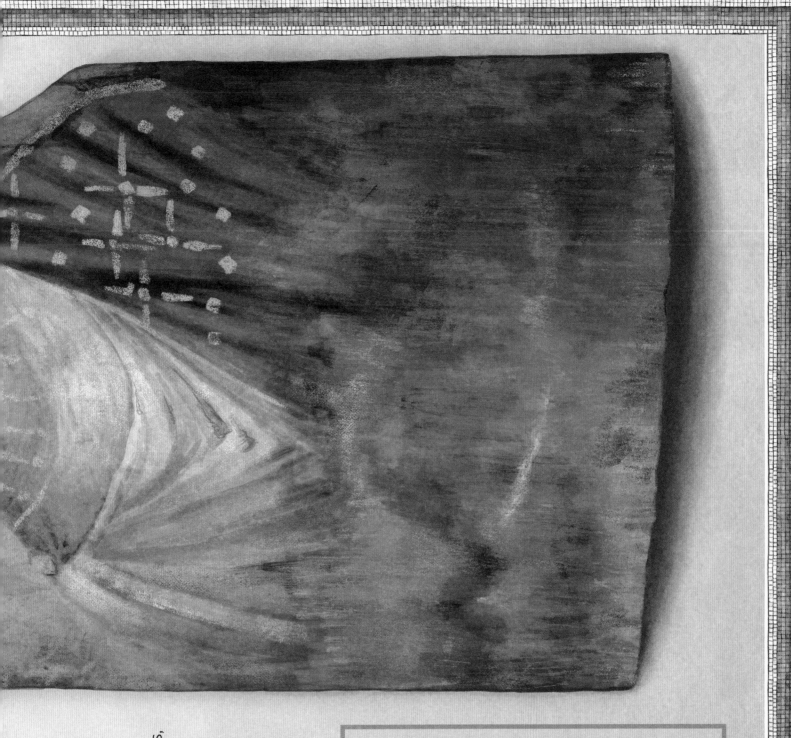

We can tell the girl came from a wealthy family. She wears valuable gold earrings and a gold necklace. The artist has used expensive gold leaf for her jewelry, wreath, clothes, and lips.

The girl would not have worn a gold wreath when she was alive. The artist added it to her mummy portrait to help celebrate her life.

FACT FILE

Discovered: Hawara, Egypt

Found today: Cleveland Museum of Art, Cleveland, Ohio, USA

Date: Around 25–37 CE

Materials: Wood, beeswax, colored pigment, gold leaf

Size: 15½ in (39.4 cm) high, 6¾ in (17.4 cm) wide

GODDESS OF HEALING

- This shimmering bronze is the head of Sulis Minerva, the goddess of wisdom and healing.

- The head is covered in gold leaf and is larger than a real-life woman's head.

- The statue sat in a huge temple in Aquae Sulis in England. Only priests were allowed to enter this holy space. Worshippers gathered in the courtyard outside, where they built altars and made sacrifices.

- Sulis Minerva's temple was next to a sacred spring, which fed public baths. Every Roman town had its own baths. People visited them not only to get clean but also to meet friends, exercise, and play games.

- Before the Romans invaded Britain, a goddess called Sul had been worshipped at the site of Sulis Minerva's temple. Sulis Minerva was a combination of Sul and the Roman goddess of wisdom, Minerva.

- Hidden beneath the statue's hairline are several small holes. These once held rivets to fix a tall warrior's helmet to Sulis Minerva's head.

- One hundred and thirty "curse tablets" were discovered at the site of Sulis Minerva's temple. People wrote to the goddess to beg for the return of stolen goods, and to ask for curses to be placed on the thieves.

FACT FILE

Discovered: Bath, UK

Found today: Roman Baths, Bath, UK

Date: 60–100 CE

Materials: Bronze, gold leaf

Size: 9¾ in (24.8 cm) high

THE MARBLE COFFIN

This stone coffin, or sarcophagus, was created for a child from a wealthy family. It is made from marble.

Death in childhood was common. Even Romans who survived to become adults frequently died before the age of 50.

The first Romans burnt their dead and put the ashes in pots called urns. The urns were then placed in pits or family tombs. Later, Romans buried their dead. Only the very rich could afford coffins like this one.

This happy scene is how the child's family wanted to remember them. The carving shows a group of boys and girls playing with walnuts. It looks like a modern game of marbles—one boy tries to knock over a pile of nuts.

- One boy is pulling another child's hair. Perhaps they are fighting over the walnuts. This reminds us that Roman children were similar to children today.

- This coffin was buried in a cemetery outside Rome's city walls. Only important people, such as emperors and generals, were buried inside the city.

- Inside the coffin, there may have been a coin in the child's mouth. This was to pay the ferryman to row the child's spirit across the river Styx, the only way it could reach the underworld safely.

FACT FILE

Discovered: Appian Way, Rome, Italy

Found today: Chiaramonti Museum, Vatican Museums, Rome, Italy

Date: About 250 CE

Materials: Marble

Size: 17 in (43 cm) high, 42¼ in (107.5 cm) long, 14¼ in (36 cm) deep

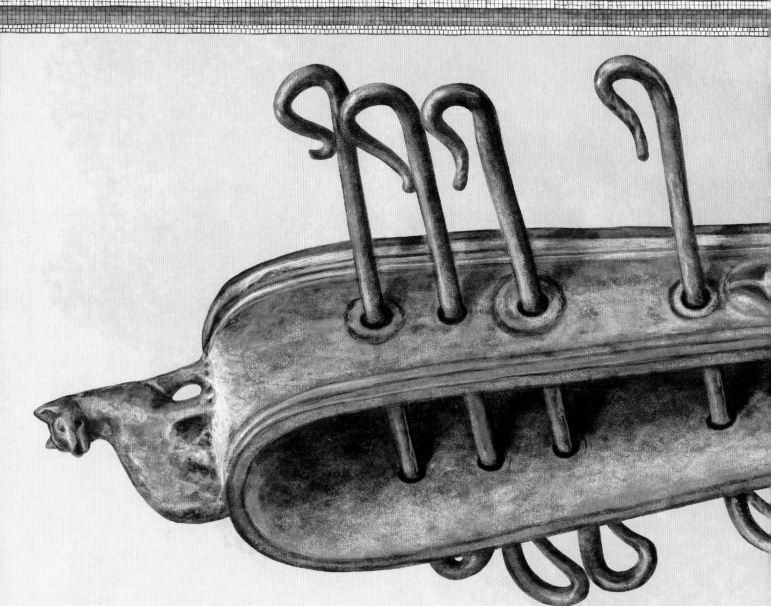

BRONZE RATTLE

🏛 This bronze musical instrument is a sistrum, which is a type of rattle. It was used in Roman religious processions and ceremonies, including funerals.

🏛 This sistrum is made of a loop of bronze attached to a handle. Metal bars are threaded loosely through holes in the frame. The bars rattle when the instrument is shaken.

🏛 Sometimes small disks were hung from each of the bars. They created a jangling noise a bit like that of a tambourine.

🏛 This type of rattle came to Rome from ancient Egypt, where it was important in the worship of the goddess Isis. When the worship of Isis spread to the Roman world, so did the use of this instrument.

The sistrum is a percussion instrument. The Romans used many other percussion instruments, including cymbals, castanets, and the *scabellum*, which was played with the feet.

The Romans believed the sistrum's rattling sound could keep evil spirits away.

FACT FILE

Discovered: Rome, Italy

Found today: British Museum, London, UK

Date: 1–200 CE

Materials: Bronze

Size: 9 in (22.9 cm) high

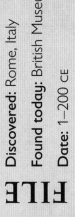

THE IMPERIAL FAMILY

🏛 Emperor Septimius Severus and his family gaze at us from this picture. It is the only painting of a Roman emperor and his family that still exists today.

🏛 The emperor is shown with his wife, Julia Domna, and their sons, Geta and Caracalla. Geta's face has been scraped off. Caracalla was jealous of his younger brother, who was murdered after their father's death. Caracalla had all pictures and statues of Geta destroyed.

🏛 Severus was the first Roman emperor born in Africa. He came from an ordinary background, but his ambition and determination helped him to rise to the top.

🏛 Julia Domna was one of the most powerful women in Roman history. Her husband may have been emperor, but she influenced many of his decisions.

🏛 Roman hairstyles changed frequently. This picture shows how Julia Domna wore her hair in heavy folds. We know the look was copied because dolls have been discovered with the same hairstyle.

🏛 All the family wear expensive clothes. The emperor and his sons have gold crowns with large gems, and carry ivory rods, or scepters. The empress wears a pearl necklace and earrings, along with a gold-and-pearl crown.

FACT FILE

Discovered: Egypt

Found today: Altes Museum, Berlin, Germany

Date: About 200 CE

Materials: Wood, paint

Size: 12 in (30.5 cm) wide

THE LYRE OF ORPHEUS

🏛 This mosaic shows the great poet and musician Orpheus. Myths tell how his singing and playing were so beautiful that even wild animals were enchanted.

🏛 Orpheus plucks the strings of his lyre. A leopard, a lion, and a boar stop to listen to the music.

🏛 This mosaic was part of a floor discovered in Tarsus, Turkey. Tarsus was an important city in the Roman Empire, and a great place of culture and learning.

🏛 Brightly colored mosaics of Orpheus have been found all over the Roman world, usually in large villas. The red and yellow details are made of glass, and are almost as vivid today as when they were laid more than 1,500 years ago.

🏛 The mosaic reminds us that the Romans loved music. It was played in religious ceremonies, at public events like gladiator contests, and in people's homes.

FACT FILE

Discovered: Tarsus, Turkey

Found today: Hatay Archaeology Museum, Antioch, Turkey

Date: About 275–300 CE

Materials: Stone and glass

Size: 64 in (162.5 cm) high, 60 in (152.5 cm) wide

BEAUTY SET

Beauty and cleanliness were very important to the Romans. Both men and women took great care over their appearance. This grooming set probably belonged to a wealthy Roman woman.

The long tool at the bottom was used to clean nails. The tool with the tiny round spoon was for scooping out earwax.

The tweezers in this set look just like modern ones. They were mainly used for plucking body hair. The Romans also used razors and pumice stones to remove unwanted hair.

Most Romans visited large public baths to wash. Few were rich enough to have their own bath at home, and it was only the very wealthy who could afford an expensive grooming set like this one.

The beauty set hung from a fine brooch pinned to a lady's waist. It showed off how wealthy she was, and how much pride she took in her appearance.

The brooch is decorated with blue and yellow enamel, a type of glass coating. Enamel was often used to add color to metal objects.

FACT FILE

Discovered: British Isles

Found today: British Museum, London, UK

Date: 43–410 CE

Materials: Copper alloy and enamel

Size: 4¼ in (10.7 cm) long, 1¾ in (4.6 cm) wide, ½ in (1.5 cm) deep

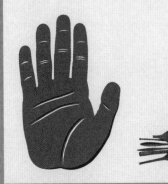

THE EMPEROR'S GUARD

Rome's mighty army had the best-trained and best-equipped soldiers in the world. They conquered a vast empire, which stretched from Britain to West Asia and North Africa.

The legionaries shown on this carving were the emperor's protectors. They formed part of a special unit called the Praetorian Guard.

Two of the soldiers wear a belt, or *balteus*. The belt's decorated leather strips were often weighed down with heavy pendants. A soldier's *balteus* showed his position in the army and provided extra protection in battle.

A Roman soldier's helmet covered the head, face, and neck. A crested helmet showed that they were an important officer.

The soldiers carry oval-shaped shields, which are painted with striking thunderbolts and eagle wings.

This sculpture was once part of the Arch of Claudius in Rome. The arch was built to celebrate Emperor Claudius's successful invasion of Britain.

FACT FILE

Discovered: Rome, Italy

Found today: Louvre-Lens Museum, Lens, France

Date: 51–52 CE

Materials: Marble

Size: 64¼ in (163 cm) high, 52¾ in (134 cm) wide, 11 in (28 cm) deep

GODDESS OF CHANCE

🏛 The Romans believed gods and goddesses watched over every part of their lives. This shiny little statue is the goddess Tutela. People prayed to her for protection and good luck.

🏛 Tutela holds a double "horn of plenty" in her left hand. Myths told how the horn belonged to a female goat that looked after the god Jupiter as a baby. Jupiter gave the horn magical powers so it would always be filled with delicious things to eat.

🏛 The heads of the twin brothers Castor and Pollux sit on the goddess's wings, just above her crown. The Romans believed the brothers gave protection to warriors in battle and sailors at sea.

🏛 The round dish in the goddess's right hand is called a patera. It was used to pour wine, milk, or oil as a gift to the gods.

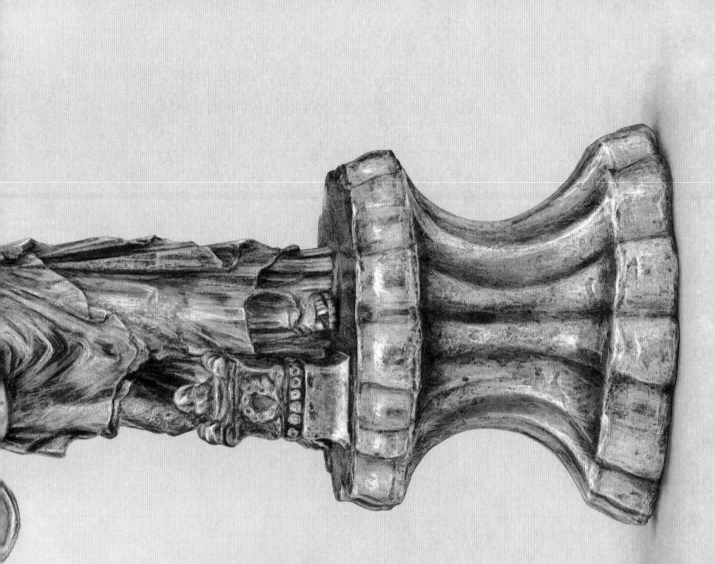

The later Romans named the days of the week after seven gods. Their heads are at the top of this statue. The first is Saturn, who gave his name to Saturday.

Statues of other gods and goddesses were discovered with this one. They were probably placed together on a shrine where they could be worshipped by the people living nearby.

FACT FILE

Discovered: Mâcon, France

Found today: British Museum, London, UK

Date: 150–220 CE

Materials: Silver, gold

Size: 5½ in (13.9 cm) high, 2¼ in (6 cm) wide, 1¾ in (4.2 cm) deep

THEATER MASK

🏛 The Romans loved to go to the theatre. The actors they saw on stage often performed wearing masks. This is a Roman model of a theater mask.

🏛 Theater masks helped the audience to instantly understand a character's personality or mood. This mask shows the unhappy face of a tragic female character.

🏛 Actors wore masks made of leather, stiff linen, or cork. This clay mask was too heavy to wear, but perhaps it decorated part of a theater.

🏛 Almost all actors were men. Masks were useful because they allowed male actors to play female characters. An actor could also play more than one role by switching their mask.

🏛 Wealthy women had slaves to arrange and style their hair. The complicated plaits on this mask took several hours to do in real life.

🏛 Masked Roman actors performed in open-air, semicircle-shaped theaters. Audiences cheered for their favorites, and booed and hissed when they did not like an actor. Sometimes they threw rotten food at the stage.

🏛 Some Roman theaters were huge. The Theatre of Pompey in the city of Rome had room for at least 11,000 spectators.

FACT FILE

Discovered: Rome, Italy

Found today: British Museum, London, UK

Date: 1–200 CE

Materials: Terracotta

Size: 8½ in (21.6 cm) high

WAR AT SEA

The Romans are most famous for their mighty army, but they also had a strong navy. This wall painting shows Roman warships in battle.

A Roman warship was lightweight and fast-moving. It carried up to 300 oarsmen. They are shown driving the ships forward with their powerful rowing in this painting.

The painting probably shows a scene from the Battle of Actium. In this battle, the Roman leader Octavian defeated the Roman general Mark Antony and the Egyptian queen Cleopatra. After his victory, Octavian became known as Augustus.

At the front of each warship is a bronze battering ram, which was used to pound, pierce, and sink enemy ships.

 This painting was discovered in one of Pompeii's finest homes. It belonged to two brothers who had once been slaves, but became wealthy merchants.

 The Romans liked to stage spectacular mock sea battles in huge stadiums. They flooded arenas with water, and made slaves and prisoners sail the ships. Many were injured or even killed in these shows.

FACT FILE

Discovered: Pompeii, Italy

Found today: House of the Vettii, Pompeii, Italy

Date: 62–79 CE

Materials: Paint, plaster

Size: Approx. 23½ in (60 cm) wide

THE GOLDEN HOARD

🏛 For centuries, these shiny gold coins lay buried under the soil of a farmer's field. They were found by a man searching for a missing hammer with a metal detector.

🏛 These coins are part of a huge treasure called the Hoxne Hoard.

🏛 The coins were made toward the end of the Roman Empire. At that time, the Romans were often at war with foreign tribes, who they called barbarians. Perhaps a wealthy family tried to hide the coins from the barbarians.

🏛 Emperor Honorius is shown on the coins. During his reign, a group of people known as the Visigoths invaded the city of Rome. They stole its treasures and killed many of its citizens.

🏛 On the back of the coins, Emperor Honorius stands with one foot on a prisoner. In his left hand, he holds a globe with a winged figure representing victory on it. This was meant to show his power and might.

🏛 There is Latin writing on the front of the coins. It tells us that Emperor Honorius is "blessed by the gods." The "RV" on the back stands for the Italian city of Ravenna, where the coins were made.

FACT FILE

Discovered: Hoxne, UK

Found today: British Museum, London, UK

Date: 402–406 CE

Materials: Gold

Size: Approx. ¾ in (2 cm) wide; 0.16 oz (4.47 g) weight

Roman coins were made from copper, bronze, silver, and gold. In early times, the Romans put pictures of their gods and goddesses on them. In later times, coins showed the faces of ruling emperors.

The first Roman coins were made at the Temple of Juno Moneta in the city of Rome. Juno Moneta was the goddess of money. *Moneta* is where the English word "money" comes from.

GOD OF WAR

▤ This colossal statue is Mars, the Roman god of war. He stands armed and ready for battle.

▤ The Romans worshipped dozens of gods and goddesses. Mars was the son of the king of the gods, Jupiter. His mother was Juno, protector of Rome.

▤ The Romans were proud of their might in warfare, and Mars was one of their most important gods. Soldiers across the empire prayed to him for protection in battle and made sacrifices to him after victory.

▤ The month of March is named after Mars. Festivals with sacrifices and horse races were held to honor him at this time of year.

▤ Mars is dressed as a soldier. He wears a short tunic, breastplate, helmet, and military cloak. His right hand is raised to grip a spear, while his other hand holds a heavy shield.

- In the middle of the breastplate are two griffins. These mythical creatures were half lion and half eagle. They represent cunning and wisdom.

- The head of Medusa is shown on Mars's chest. People thought the face of this snake-haired monster could keep evil away.

- Mars wears lion-headed boots on his feet. The fierce lion was a symbol of strength and courage.

FACT FILE

Discovered: Rome, Italy

Found today: Capitoline Museums, Rome, Italy

Date: 100–138 CE

Materials: Marble

Size: 11 ft 10 in (3.6 m) high

LITTLE WOODEN HORSE

🏛 Many Roman children enjoyed playing with simple toys like this little horse on wheels. It's easy to imagine it being pulled over the bumps and cracks in the ground.

🏛 A piece of string was threaded through the horse's nose so that it could be pulled along.

🏛 As well as pull toys like this one, Roman children played with balls, dolls, toy weapons, hoops, scooters, yo-yos, and marbles. Toys were usually homemade rather than bought in shops.

🏛 Poorer Roman children might not have had many toys, or time to play with them. Some were sent to work at a young age. A girl could even be married from the age of twelve.

FACT FILE

Discovered: Akhmim, Egypt

Found today: British Museum, London, UK

Date: 1–300 CE

Materials: Wood, paint

Size: 3 in (7.6 cm) high, 4½ in (11.5 cm) wide, 2¾ in (7 cm) deep

This little horse was discovered in Egypt. The Romans conquered Egypt and ruled there for hundreds of years.

The medicines we have today did not exist in Roman times. Smallpox, measles, and other diseases killed many children. Grieving parents sometimes buried their young with a favorite toy, like this wooden horse.

HOUSEHOLD GODS

Most Roman homes had a shrine dedicated to the gods and spirits that watched over the family. People prayed to them for guidance and protection. This shrine was discovered in the ruins of a house in the ancient city of Pompeii.

The shrine, or *lararium*, is in the shape of a small temple. The two figures dancing on tiptoe are household gods. They are holding up drinking horns.

In Roman times, it was thought that each person had their own special spirit to guide them. The figure in the center is the house owner's protective spirit. It is wearing a white toga.

The Romans believed that the spirits of their dead ancestors also watched over them. They took care to remember their ancestors at the household shrine, and regularly visited their graves.

People offered gifts to their household gods. They would lay grain, honey cakes, fruit, wine, or incense at the shrine.

At the bottom of the shrine, a bearded serpent slithers through the grass. The Romans saw the snake as a symbol of wisdom and good fortune. It was thought to bring luck to the home.

FACT FILE

Discovered: Pompeii, Italy

Found today: House of the Vettii, Pompeii, Italy

Date: 62–79 CE

Materials: Paint on plaster

Size: Approx. 78¾ in (200 cm) wide

THE SWORD OF TIBERIUS

🏛 This famous sword and its sheath were discovered in the river Rhine in Germany, an area of many fierce ancient Roman battles.

🏛 The sword was a Roman soldier's main weapon, especially in close-up combat. It could be drawn quickly from straps on his right side.

🏛 This sword probably belonged to an important officer. Perhaps it was made to celebrate a great victory.

🏛 The gleaming scabbard is in much better condition than the blade. It looks gold or silver, but in fact it is made from brass coated with tin. The scabbard protected the blade when it was not in use.

🏛 The engraving at the bottom of the scabbard shows a female warrior armed with an axe. She probably represents the defeated enemy.

Many experts believe the seated figure at the top of the scabbard is Emperor Tiberius. He is presenting his nephew Germanicus with a statue of the goddess Victory. Germanicus commanded the Roman army in the part of Germany where the sword was found.

FACT FILE

Discovered: Mainz, Germany

Found today: British Museum, London, UK

Date: 15 CE

Materials: Iron, bronze, tin

Size: Blade 22½ in (57.5 cm) long, 2¾ in (7 cm) wide; scabbard 23 in (58.5 cm) long, 3½ in (8.7 cm) wide

THE ROMAN EMPIRE

Rome

Pompeii

GERMANIA

GAUL

HISPANIA

Londinium

Rome

Pompeii

Carthage

ILLYRIA

Athens

AFRICA

MEDITERRANEAN SEA

BLACK SEA

ASIA

SYRIA

Jerusalem

Alexandria

EGYPT

PARTHIA

This map shows the Roman Empire in 117 CE, at the height of its power.

N
W   E
S